GROWING PAINS

GROWING PAINS

Lauren Rose Lenyi

RESOURCE *Publications* · Eugene, Oregon

GROWING PAINS

Resource Publications
An Imprint of Wipf and Stock Publishers
199 W. 8th Ave., Suite 3
Eugene, OR 97401

www.wipfandstock.com

PAPERBACK ISBN: 978-1-6667-7884-7
HARDCOVER ISBN: 978-1-6667-7885-4
EBOOK ISBN: 978-1-6667-7886-1

To Grandpa,

You are the reason I strive to be better than I am.

Contents

Dear Reader,

Growing up I felt alone, mistaken, and like the singular black sheep of the world. Later, I learned that most people feel this way when growing up, but few still think this as adults. I cannot decide which category I fall into; I suppose I'll let you decide. However, I do know one thing: growing pains have shaped me into the person I am today. I have endured it all and I can confidently say that the pain will subside and leave you with indescribable pleasures. I hope you see that too.

With Love,
Lauren Lenyi

PROLOGUE

Speak

Tell me your story and I'll tell you mine.
I'll listen to your voice
As it makes its way
Through my mind.
I'll pay close attention
And give my utmost respect.
For your story is important,
Even though I don't know it yet.

It could be sad, joyful,
Odd, or complex.
Whatever it may be,
I'll listen with hearty intent.
Prose or lulls,
Short or long,
Do tell your tale,
My friend,
I want it all.

Once you've said your last words,
Drawn in a deep breath,
Let yourself take a break
And I'll sing my tragedy next.

My story flows from me.
Free and true
And as I speak I think,
Will you judge me for it
As I do too?

Will you detest my stories?
Will you forget it soon?

Or will you give me
The same respect,
That I bestowed to you?

Tell me your story and I'll tell you mine.
A fair enough trade if you have the time.

IDENTITY

Sit, Stay, Submit

Conformity is a concept
Conceived by society's
Incessant,
Infectious,
Insecurities.

I want self-actualization.
Not rhythmic allegiance
Out of pure convenience.

A contagious,
Complacent,
Collectively Conscious
Creation.

Yet

My boobs sag
From the burden of giving life and
Entertaining the judgments
Of life around me.

When my lips speak truth and poetry
While others hear sweet nothings.
My clothes build up my confidence,
But makes others feel
A tingling in their loins.

My body is etched
Purple with stretch marks.
From being pulled back and forth
By men who can't decide if they
Want an independent woman,
Swift and sassy.
Or an innocent little girl
They can use and abuse.
Yet. . .
Either way,

They.
Want.
Me.
Still.

sold!

My soul was sold before I was born.
I had a vagina,
Need I say more?

Purple

What the fuck is feminity and masculinity
When men once wore pink with pride
And women were adorned in hues of blue.
Such ridiculous constructs
Thrust upon us at birth.
Your expectations are a curse.
Your stereotypes maybe even worse.
So,
What are your traditions worth
When the power they hold
Is created from the same old broken mold?

Feminine guilt

I can't keep going on like this.
Being the crutch,
The shoulder to cry on,
The one to throw a stitch.
I care more about others
Then they do for themselves.
I give them the world,
When they won't even give the minimum
To anyone in return.

But when I'm spread so thin,
Like this,
I can't take care of myself.
For I'm left broken,
Shattered to bits.

I need to pull away,
To tend to my own pain.
Lean into myself
And cry it out.

I can't let it fester any longer.
My mascara runs down
Staining my cheeks.
My foundation cracks
Showing the imperfections masked
Underneath.
I explode, implode,
Sheltering nothing.
I take it all in,

Let it all out.

Still my mind can never truly understand.
Right when I think I know it all,
I get knocked off my pedestal;
And realize that there will always be something
I do not know,
That I cannot fix.
My guilt about leaving,
And taking myself in,
Does nothing but hinder me;
Confuses and curses me.

It's not my responsibility
Or duty in life,
To serve others
With a pretty pink smile,
In a lavender dress,
While I clean up
Everyone's mess.
But feminine guilt
Is a hard enemy to best.

First Blood

First blood,
Celebrate!
You're a woman now, kid.
Isn't that great?

Second blood,
You've had your first real taste.
The little girl learns
Of a woman's place.

Third blood,
You see their hate.
The boys do not mask
Their disdain.

Fourth blood,
Old news.
Switch from pads to tampons,
Your friends have done so too.

Fifth blood,
In incredible pain,
As you realize that kids
Are, allegedly, your fate.

Sixth blood,
What's new?
This time a boy
Sits hand and hand with you.

Seventh blood,
Good luck.
You forgot the condom,
Now you're fucked.

Eighth blood,
Cold sheets.
You lie there and think,
The abortion clinic smells bleak.

Ninth blood,
Stay strong, stand true.
Your mother questions
Your morality.
You begin to do so too.

Tenth blood,
Blue moon.
Wedding bells ring,
All singing for you
And the groom.

Eleventh blood,
Post honeymoon.
The inquiry begins
"When will you have kids?"
No talk about *Ifs*.
It's going to happen,
Everyone but you is sure of this.

Twelfth blood,
So quick?
Your family is disappointed

In your inability
To conceive a kid.

Thirteenth blood,
See the doctor at noon.
He says there is something wrong
With you.
You are not as sad
as you thought you would be.
There is worse news in the world
If only everyone else could agree.

Fourteenth blood,
No diapers to change,
Your body is to blame.
What kind of woman are you
If you cannot do
What God designed you to do?

Fifteenth blood,
Your husband resents you.
The doctor pities you.
Now your family doesn't believe
Anything you say is true.

Sixteenth blood,
You're still young
Yet time is running out.
The life in your hands
Has slowly bled out.

Seventeenth blood,
The orphanage is packed,

Stacked with the unwelcome.
You see a blue-eyed boy.
A toddler of three,
The baby you could never have.
You're the mother he needs.

Eighteenth blood,
You are taken by surprise,
When your new son cries
As he sees
Your scarlet-stained thighs.

Nineteenth blood,
There isn't much to say.
The doctor said it can leave any day.
You've run out of tampons,
Does it matter anyways?

Twentieth blood,
The last few drops.
A woman once fruitful
Now barren and lost.

You welcome the end.
You are not sad it's gone.
Just fearful of people
Who, no doubt will share
Their unwanted thoughts.

To this I say
Just remember your strength.
You are a woman,
Either way,

There is no reason
To be ashamed.

<u>Bride-to-be</u>

Beautiful bride-to-be,
Perfect white teeth,
Pristine sexual history.
With a flawless sense of style,
She wouldn't dare
Make the boys go wild.

Beautiful bride-to-be,
With the ideal body type
To have children once or twice
And bounce back in the nick of time.

Beautiful bride-to-be,
Smart and independent
But chooses to follow love
Or whatever her man needs.
Classy yet fun,
A blast to be around
When the boys have left town.

Beautiful bride-to-be,
She's not like the other girls.
She has a mind of her own.
Unique and gorgeous,
Never prancing around in skimpy clothes.
No cleavage
Nor Fishnet treasure troves.

Beautiful bride-to-be,
She is everything Man

Has fantasized her to be.
Cute in public
And sexy behind closed doors.
Her pouty lips and flared hips
Make her man hard
Quick.

Our Bride with big, kind eyes
Glittering with childlike glee.
Buzzing about in her wedding room suite.
She had dreamed of this day,
Draped in silk and lace.
Today she will say,

"I do."

Oh, Sweet, little bride-to-be,
Only *18*.

Excuse, me

I wasn't there.
It wasn't me.
I would never have supported
Them,
Their beliefs.

Okay . . .

Thanks for using me
As the perfect vessel to
To absolve the guilt
I did not build.

Star Spangled Banner

I hold my necklace,
My Star of David,
In the palm of my hand.
Squeezing and pressing
Till it leaves an imprint
But not just on my hand.

Jewish Girl

I did not grow up
With a great understanding of our past.
Just a warning
To never fight back,
To not react.

I was not supposed to talk about it in school.
I was lucky to have blonde hair
But my nose gave them a chance
To speculate, to express their hate,
In passive-aggressive ways.

I still remember the times
When people would blurt out
Whatever was on their minds.
I was told my nose reminded them
Of Anne Frank.
A scared little girl
Who died alone,
Poisoned by hate.
What was I to say?
"Thanks?"

In social studies,
My brother was told
That Hitler would have loved him.
Who says that to a nine-year-old?
Evidently, a teacher would.

My father was bullied as a small child

So, they hid their menorah,
Not just for a little while.
So far from N.Y.,
Now hiding from prying eyes.
I guess we'll celebrate Christmas
For the rest of our lives.

It's moments like this
Where I miss my Great Grandfather.
He stood by my side.
He would never run or hide.
And he always
Wore his big nose with pride.

As I grew up
I learned what defines
This is my history of mine.

I refuse to let history repeat itself.
I reclaimed my truth.
Now, I will not stand down,
Because
Against all odds
We picked ourselves up and
Wore our stars on our hearts.
And continued on
Despite our battle scars.

<u>under the shade of canopied trees</u>

I fell in love with women
Under the shade of canopied trees.
Breathing in the scent of pine and peaches,
Eve hand in hand with Eve.

Trying to find the same message
In her eyes,
That I know danced within mine.

Dimpled smiles
And flushed cheeks
Never fail to unravel me.

Though my feelings are true,
It is hard to express
This kind of love.
When the responses
Come from places of
Indifference, ignorance,
Or religious deliverance.

If I speak what will become of me,
The woman I love,
And the shining pair
That we could have been?
Yet, I cling to the hope that one day,
I could be.
Be with a woman who is eager
To start a perfectly queer life
Alongside me.

Insert Title [Here]

An adorable baby girl.
A cute little girl.
A bright little lady.
A mature young lady.
A promising young woman.
A gorgeous woman.
A boy magnet.
A bossy feminist.
A drama queen.
A diva.
A babe.
A sexy bitch.
A bimbo.
A tease.
A slut.
A whore.
A jealous girlfriend.
A needy wife.
A pregnant lady.
A mother.
A milf.
A cougar.
A prude.
A woman going gray.
A crazy Grandma.
A cute old cat lady.
An honorable woman.
A dead woman.
A woman . . .

A girl . . .
A female . . .
A. Cunt.

Crave

I tell you I am a writer,
That word does not convey
What I cannot say.

I am a fiend with a keyboard.
Bored,
Alone,
Scared.
Clawing through my skin,
Trying
To detect a heartbeat within
Or a soul to dissect
So that these words
Will have meaning.
Or at least no hollowness to detect.
But more than anything,
I need to make you feel
Something.

I need to see you, reacting, interacting
With a piece of me
Or at least who I desire to be.
I must earn the validation
I will never gain
Through my self-inflicted seclusion,
Contusions, and delusions.

I need to know what you think
And study your thoughts
To learn

How to identify
My own worth and beauty
If indeed,
There is any left to perceive.

This is what it is
To be a writer.
A freak sinking
Into their own morality
And mortality.
A girl whose only goal
Is to be seen in utter totality.

CHILDHOOD

<u>Gray</u>

I wish someone had warned me
Not how different
Life becomes
Once you grow up.
But the fact that we
Are expected to leave behind
Our childhood
In favor of adulthood.

Everyone proclaims
Neverland is fake
Or that Wonderland isn't real.
When instead they
Should tell us to enjoy our time
With the lost boys,
Hand in hand.
And appreciate gossiping
With beautiful mermaids
Who grace us
With their momentary presence on the land.

Or
To relish the days we spend
Painting the roses,
Drinking some tea
Before we go back and go mad
As we soon realize,
We wouldn't ever be allowed back in Wonderland.
That we will be too old for Neverland.

But do not negate our happy reality,
To prove that in a few years' time
The real world will eat us alive.

You're Next

Some days I look my age.
On other days I appear quite young.
The punchline here
Has nothing to do with my choices.
Because my individuality
Or personality is irrelevant
In this scenario.

They simply want me as they see me.
Whether I look like a grown woman
Or a child.
For their fantasies,
Ones I refuse to fulfill.

I was only fourteen
The moment I realized this.
Right then a chill ran up my spine,
Like a clammy hand
Tracing up to the nape of my neck.
It's still there from time to time
And if you don't feel it yet, girl. . .
Well,
You're next in line.

Pray

God,
Can I get a new toy for my birthday?
God,
Can I have a doggy for Christmas?
God,
Will you tell Mom to let me see this movie tonight?
God,
Can I have some nice friends?
God,
Why do boys break my heart?
God,
Why do I like girls?
God,
Why did you take my friend away at such a young age?
God,
Why are so many people sick?
God,
Why must we live in pain?
God,
We are your children, but why do we not feel like siblings?
God,
Why are people murdering each other in your name?
God,
I hate to ask this but
Why should I pray to you when you provide no change?

<u>Missing</u>

I miss the days
Where music was played
From dusk till daybreak.
When human connection
Was more than a reflection
Of blue light and misdirection.

I miss the days
When the truth was discovered,
Not created to gain acclaim,
However depraved.
When boys and girls could be friends
Without others implying another end.

I miss the days when my voice would echo
And my words were received
With a hearty laugh.
Now all I see are the double clicks,
The hashtags and follows.

I miss the days
When we weren't all so sick.

<u>I got you</u>

Into the dark,
Dank woods
Across the lake,
Beyond the rocky hillside.

Past the grazing fawns,
Down the rough
Man-made trail
And into the quaint,
Cozy hut.

There you will find,
Something hidden inside.
I'll give you a hint,
And let you in
To find my little secret . . .

Have you found it yet?

It's all the fucks I do not give.

Sorry

"This isn't right."
Oh, baby, it's never been right.
Sorry to disappoint,
But have a good life.

Mute

Contemplative silence,
I've learned,
Is more powerful than
Quick ill-intended words.

LOVE

Question

Am I the problem
Or do I just fall for the problem?

Could and Would

If I could go back
And tell you that I will always love you,
No matter what you do,
How far you stray,
Or the countless nights
Your actions have made me enraged.
Would you believe me then?
Would you change for the better
To keep your best friend?
So that this poem,
Our story,
Will have a different end.

Heartwarming, heartbreaking

Love and infatuation
Are here to destroy me.
I know they are not the same,
Still, I cannot differentiate
The key factor
That sets them apart.
They are both infuriating and lovely.
Heartwarming, and heartbreaking.
Equally annoying and thrilling.
Both villains and heroes.
Fire and ice.
Yet I can't tell which is which.
Regardless I'm petrified.

<u>You</u>

My body has been starved for so long.
During the day I forget what love feels like.
At night I begin to reminisce about its respite.

In my dreams, it is a fond friend,
The faceless, nameless *You.*
You, I feel, are Love.
A love for in my waking hours,
I know nothing of.
One for which I yearn so desperately.
Not a person.
Rather
An emotion, a feeling,
A state of being.
A dream I never want to wake from.

I long to stay with this mythical Love
Because in reality,
I am unsure
What depth of love
I'm capable of.

Long and Short, Too

Together we lay
For only a little while.
Short enough
For my sheets to smell like you.
Long enough
That the sound of the door closing
Hurts us both.
Long enough for my heart to break
And short enough for your delicate whispers
To sink far into my brain.
I longed for your essence then,
And I still do today.
I'm not sure if that will go away.
I'm not sure I want that to change.

Goodbye

When we kissed for the first time
I didn't get the right kind of butterflies.
No sparkle arose in my eye.
My smile was not wide
But melancholy,
Devoid of the sublime.
I was saddened
As I realized
It would be the
First,
Last,
And only time . . .
Farewell,
My sweet little sorrow.
Farewell and goodbye.

<u>For You</u>

Nothing prepares you
For *that* feeling.
There are no rom-coms
True to life,
Nor any books
Whose prose or protagonists
Can explain the air we share.

I do not dare try
And put it in words
Far bigger than me
Or greater than that feeling.
I know I am unable to do it justice.

All I can say
Is books, movies,
Shows, and plays
Will never be enough.
After having a taste
You know there is nothing sweeter.
It's an addiction, a disease,
With no treatment or cure,
As if one would want it anyhow.
Because nothing
can ever come close to the feeling,

Of

F
  a
   l
    l
     i
      n
       g

For

You.

...

Our Love Language is
One of silence
That only we can read.
An entanglement of thoughts
Never spoken
Only seen
In both our eyes
Caverns of wrath
And mystery.

A mutual understanding
We both know to be true as
When I listen to my own heartbeat
All I can think about
Is *youyouyou*.
No need to speak,
I know you feel it too.

I can tell by the smiles
On our faces
That we are hopeless to subdue,
Even in a crowded room
We are the only two.

People disappear,
The noise fades soon
And we are left
In silence.
A succession of ellipsis.
It's a pure
performance of love

That connects me
To you.

<u>Silence</u>

Our love language is still silence.
The silence in the air when
I ask you what's wrong
And you say

Don't worry about it. I'm fine.
The sting of silence flares inside when
I think back to the time,
Where you were my sole kernel of light.

I can deal with being left on read
Or having you decline my calls.
But what breaks me in two is
Your empty words.
As they are far worse
Than silence.

There is no communication.
No shy glances from across the room.
Our smiles aren't mirrored
And our hearts beat
To no known tune.

When you speak
Your words do not ring true.
Nevertheless, I can see,
A storm cloud creeping closer
And closer.
Eventually, it will thunder,
Rain,

And evaporate.
Leaving our unspoken words,
Our contempt,

Ourselves.
Floating in the air
And even more

Silence.

Mr. & Mrs.

I am grateful for the quietness we shared
As it taught me the difference between
Silence and tranquility.
I was well acquainted with
A comfortable kind of stillness.
However, this was an abyss
That I helped expand
Through my submissive state
And my subservient bliss
That you fell for oh, so quick.

But I never knew tranquility
When I was with you.
If I was Mrs. Congeniality
You were Mr. Immorality.
Keeping me from enjoying
My sweet somethings
To stop and taste your sour nothings.
I've left your bitter breath behind
And now I hold both
Tranquility and silence close.
Still, with gratitude,
I toast to you.
For teaching me
The true meaning
Of Apathy.

Heart Attack

Love is whatever you need it to be.
Whatever delusion you want it to be.
That doesn't mean it's real.
That doesn't mean that feeling you get,
The butterflies,
That electric hum,
Or breath stuck
Trying to flee your lungs
Is true, Love.

It is a lovesick heart attack.
Thumping, pulsing,
Numbing you
From the inside out.
Your heart is reacting
To something new,
Good or bad?
Merely a warning.
It is up to you
To choose.
Because when the heart attacks,
It breaks too.
I tell you this
Because I love you.

DOUBT

Deviation

Everything is changing.
For the best,
For the worst.
But what do I do,
When I can't tell which is which?

Do I want things to change,
Or rather stay the same?
Will the change make me forget,
Or allow me to evolve?
I still don't know what to expect.
I hate surprises,
Though if I look hard enough,
Will I discover,
That what lies next,
Is really no secret?

Did I know what would happen all along?
Or was I just there for the ride?
Blind, deaf, and hopeless
To my downfall.
Do I say a prayer or pave the way
For the mistakes and triumphs
That lay in wait?

I don't know
Do I let what will be, be?
Or do I go against fate,
And create my own way?
Everything is changing,

Everything is the same.
Everything is good,
Everything is bad,
Everything is a mystery,
And everything is right in front of my face,
Screaming and whispering to me,

"Not everything has to be okay."

Double Trouble

Panic attacks, while being locked inside,
Double the pain and absolve all pride.

Certain

Depression and Anxiety
Are worse when you're certain
You are cursed.

1 to 10

How human do you feel,
On a scale from one to ten?
I don't think I'll ever know
What a perfect ten feels like.
My mind cannot even fully comprehend
The idea that somehow,
Someway,
I will wholeheartedly feel connected
To this time and place.

There are billions of humans
Like me, all playing
A pre-dictated
Fucked up a game of Monopoly.
Interacting with each other,
Killing,
Loving,
Cussing out others.
A game in which
No one ever wins.
And yet,
Some people feel like a ten out of ten,
As human as can be apparently.
Is that really a good thing?

Pity Party

I wish I could do things
That others take for granted.
If only to make people think
About how precious
Their perfect lives can be.

Acknowledge your comfort and ignorance,
Please.
So I can finally leave
My self-centered pity party.
This sturdy trap
That is simply,

Me.

Feeling?

I cannot differentiate
Contentedness and numbness.
I've felt everything for so long.
Now
I don't know what to think
Of the fall,
Of it all.

Do I face each scenario with grace?
Or turn the other way
To save myself from losing face?
True, it is my life and
I get to choose where it will go,
But how will I know?
I don't.

I don't know

I don't know

This terrifies me the most.

Procrastination:

One more time,
And then i'll get my ass in line.
One more dime,
Then i'll save it next time.
One more smile,
And then i'll rest for a while.
One more piece,
Then i'll stop eating this week.
One more video,
Then i'll write this thing.
One more teardrop,
Then I'll be fine.
One more lie
And I'll stop procrastinating. . .
I'm sure of it this time.

<u>each and every kind</u>

Can I trust you?
Do I want to?
What am I thinking?
What can I create?
I don't even trust myself
To write this on the page.

It's hard to write,
When your work cannot be read.
"It's too emotional,
too dark,"
But that's not what I said.
My words are meant to be read.
Meant to be consumed.
But will they judge me?
Will I judge you?

I create from my soul
And I try to please you,
Really I do.
Yet, I cannot help but speculate,
Your next move.
Will you cry?
Will you criticize?
Will you erase it from your mind?
Can I deal with the reactions?
Each and every kind?
I need to write, I have to.
And I want this to be read,

I do.

I'm just scared
Of whatever happens next.

PAIN

Oh

My life is a comedy,
That is funny to everyone but me.

Proverbial bullshit

"Blood is thicker than water,"
But I'm not sure that's true.
I know that the tears I shed
Come all too quick and
That the crimson blood
I bleed,
Is far more profound
When family
Is orchestrating your misery
In the background.

Non-Fiction

I haven't had a dream about you in a while.
So when I did
A piece of my heart died inside,
For I realized when I saw your face
I didn't conjure you up
From a fictional place.
You still roam this Earth
Whether I am asleep or awake.

<u>Once More</u>

You know it's gotten bad
When your kitty kat brass knuckles
Become your staple jewelry.

You know it's gotten bad
When your bubblegum pink pepper spray
Overtakes your keychain.

You know it's gotten bad
When your neck is tweaked
From all the surveillance
You did this week.

You know it's gotten bad
When you can't sleep
Without double, triple checking
That you've locked your bedroom door.

You know its gotten bad
When you can feel your old scars
Split open
Burning, taunting,
And warning you
Once more.

The Facts

No one tells you
What stalking truly is.
Tv shows lie,
Courtrooms deny,
Women are urged
Not to overreact
And stick to the facts.
But,
The fact is
He
Is
Still
There.

So I'll tell you the facts
As best as I can.

He waits for me to walk out of class.
Following me down the hall
No doubt staring at my ass.

He listens in
On my conversations.
He weaseled his way
Into all of my safe spaces:
My complex,
My classes,
My clubs,
My consciousness.
Drawling in a monotone voice

With undertones

Of devious, sexual woes.

My friends took notice,
They made up a game one day
To distract me from his predatory ways.
The stare counter was created
To measure the audacity
This boy had
To swivel in his chair
A full 180 degrees
Just to stare directly at me.
The record was easy to beat,
Right now it's at 11 times an hour,
I dread to see
What it will be like next week.

And
I am sure he knows
I see him too.
I plan my escape,
Trying to stray from his gaze,
Clutching onto my friends,
Wishing for it all to end.

He knows
That I hate what he's doing.
I hate what he has done to me.
My fight or flight
Has turned into hide or die.
Yet. I say nothing
While he continues to do . . .
Something.

I talked to my friends,
They weren't shy about sharing their concerns.
They tried to convince me
That I was not a shrew
For telling the truth.

I chatted with professionals
And that is when
It hit me.
Like punch
Right to my brain,
Knocking out all the bullshit
I had been trained to believe.

I was advised
To get a restraining order.
Watch out.
Get a grip.
Call the cops if anything is amiss.
Because the fact is,
I was being stalked.
"Oh, Honey, how could you miss it?"

Invisible

I did not advocate for my body
For eighteen long years.
Though the chaos began much earlier.
It all started when I was a kid.
They knew I had problems
From the moment I was born.
I was a bad baby,
Always upset and sore.
Though everyone thought
It was a common bug,
Nothing more.

I grew up with tears,
Scarring my face.
I yelled till my voice was raw,
Turning red with anger.
On the playground
My knees were always bloody,
Though that was never my concern.
I avoided the happy-go-lucky kids
Who would go about their days
As I wish I could.
I envied them so,
The effortlessness they possessed.
I'd act up,
Go to the nurses' office.
They noticed
I was a frequent flyer and
I always left in a hurry.

We went to the doctor for the first time.

A male doctor, a family friend
Trading questions with my mother and father,
About my own life and pain,
Mine, mine, mine.
There's another valid form
That got me nowhere near a cure.

I sat at the table
Being poked and prodded.
Not to ask for my expertise,
On the subject at hand.
I was the subject at hand.

"Are you in pain?"
They asked.
At this moment no,
But I was sure that wouldn't last.
And so I left
With a generic diagnosis
Weighing on my back.
A kid who didn't understand
How to express the truth
To the individuals, the adults,
That could do what I couldn't do.

The only thing I said was,
"When will it stop?"
The doctor smiled sourly,
"When you get married, I think"
Even then I knew,
The euphemism he used
Was just to soothe,

It would never be true.

Years later,
As a teenager
The pain lingered.
Though the care for my health,
Shifted up higher.
Everything was well until it wasn't,
Just as it always goes.
Though this time my issues
We're connected, intertwined
My belly and my mind.

It was a new pain
I was not accustomed to it at first.
We went to more doctors,
They fixed my head
Rather quickly.
Slapped a bandage on
When I needed to be stitched.
I was used to the physical torment
But not so good at speaking.
My words would come out
With the vomit, a horrid noise.

And right at the start of freshman year,
A fresh kind of torture lurked near.
More than a kid, but not quite an adult,
My mother assumed
Something was up.
And I knew it too.
But in an able-bodied world,
Who was I to conclude,
That the pain I suffered

Was anything out of the blue?
It surely wasn't new.

We went to a new doctor
And though I didn't think much at the time,
The new men wanted to take a look inside.
I was wheeled in, needles in place,
Propped on a bed.
Ready to take pictures.
Microscope close,
Solving the mystery as they go.
They asked me what music I preferred,
I told them I don't care
I'd be asleep in a moment
And it wouldn't matter to me.
They were perplexed by my lack of niceties.

The tests came back,
I wasn't dying.
My insides were pink.
No cysts formed mountains or peaks.
So my pain couldn't be too bad.
Not in someone so young and healthy.
They gave me a new label:
IBSC.
A semi-sensitive stomach.
I knew that was not the whole truth.
But I went on
For years
Trusting the doctors
With a new diet,
Some pills,
And a mantra pounded into me,

"It's not so bad, smile through the pain."

Countless times I repeated only this tune,
As I lay on the bathroom floor
Unable to move.
Still, the thought was always there:
What is wrong with me?
Will anyone ever know the truth?

The diet gave me an inch.
The pills were shit.
I went on with my life
Still rotting in my painful pit.

I can be fine one minute
And struck down in less
But if I do not make my pain public,
They think it just gets suppressed.
I profess
"I'm fine, it's not so bad"
But if you walked a mile in my shoes,
You'd gasp,
collapse, and pray for it to pass.

I got into college
And a few days before my big move
I landed in the hospital,
From a UTI infection.
It was the most excruciating pain
I've experienced to this day.
My body is unique to an annoying degree
Thus the symptoms were exclusive to me.
I broke out in hives.
I cried and I cried.

I thought I would die.
Until my Mom and Dad said,
"We love you; you will be fine"
That sparked a flame inside me.
I was exhausted.
Nauseous.
Back home in my bed
I realized
For the accommodations
The school would give me
I would need to see a doctor
To examine if I deserved
A helping hand.
Though right now
I didn't even know if I could stand.

But I went back
To the doctor with the camera.
We told him what to sign.
He asked a few questions
And in my fatigue, the fog,
The shock of it all
The floodgates broke
And I spoke.
Of the never-ending loop of pain.
The circus inside me.

In a calm voice,
He branded me true:
Abdominal migraines,
Lucky you!
Well, what the fuck was that?
It's chronic pain to be exact.
Though I didn't find out till much later,

All I knew was that it justified,

What I had been feeling all my life.

He said I should have come back sooner,
I don't dwell on what could have been
Though I wondered what stopped him
During those four years
From calling
To check-in.

I was given new drugs,
They actually helped.
I was sent home
With only a bit more knowledge of myself.
And a glimmer of hope.
I promised myself
I would never lose it
As long as I live.
I'd hold onto it, near and dear.
I will not let the pain win.

I moved out,
Started my education.
I learned about writing,
Literature, and
Eventually myself.
When six months later
During a flare-up,
I wrote down all the questions I had.
I finally advocated for myself.

I talked for so long.
Making up for lost time.
Not worrying about being a bother.
I took this as a sign.
Trying to cope with the fact
That I'm not "okay"
That people to this day
Can't understand,
Don't care or believe,
That the world was not made for people like me.

Yet I advocate for my body still.
I try to be kinder to it
But it's hard to advocate for your body,
When it does not do the same for you.

I reckon with this reckoning,
Wondering why my body is the enemy.
The truth has always been hard to find,
Though I realize now it's always been inside.
Surviving the guilt,
The pain, the pleasure,
Has all made me stronger,
Helped me appreciate life.

Through
Compassion and cruelty,
And others checking my credibility
I have learned what it means
To live with an invisible disability.

<u>Burn</u>

I want to burn down the world.
Not only to start from scratch,
But to be the savior
Who stopped the flames
With her own tears.
A hero of the new world,
A legend of the old.
The very same one
That
Burned
Me
First.

DEATH

Beginning to End

You are brought into this world crying
With others in pain whispering your name,
And often our lives end in the same twisted way.

morbid reprieve

Your mother was drunk,
Irate, slurring, and spitting
On the microphone
Throughout your wake.
Your sister was an hour late
But I knew there was no traffic,
Not at that time of day.
Of course, they had every reason
To be far from okay.

Those who used to hate you
Are somehow now your best friend.
In the end, you are gone
And I hope you didn't have to see
The mortal, human mess
That manifested while we celebrated
Your life and death.
How sad is it
That I pray to God
That you're in the abyss?
How selfish am I to write this?
When I hadn't been a good friend
Toward the end.
Yet, I think about you now,
As I feel there are so few of us left.
Not many more to grieve for
And even less for grieving.
I wish the universe
Would cease this morbid reprieve.
And let you find peace.

Death

Why must all the good ones go too fast?
I wish Death would stop being selfish.
May the Grim Reaper
Leave the innocent be
And play with the souls
Who dug themselves too deep.
Don't take away those whose love
Is a beacon to the damned
Seeking to be redeemed.

Error 404

When you died
I felt ashamed,
As I still do now
For I feel almost nothing.
At most,
I feel empty when I think of you.

When you died,
All I could recall
Was the tears I shed
On your bathroom floor.
They fell freely as
You continued to pound

Pound

Pound

At the door.

I remember
The turmoil in my father's eyes
As you left him time after time.

I recall when you turned
A blind eye
To the hatred your wife threw
At my mother.
The very same despise
I now catch glimpses of

Within her eyes.

And I'm sorry to say
It was there
When you died.

I witnessed my brother's self-doubt
Increase over the years.
Because you chastised him
For being the kid he was.

He isn't that way anymore.
None of us are the same.
Our optimism has been stripped,
Our trust in you has turned to mist.

But now I still do feel
Ashamed for it all,
That you died
And I feel
Practically nothing at all.

In Memoriam,

I'm surprised we were ever told
That you died.
I cried for the ones you left behind,
Never for you.

I was not surprised, however,
That we were not told
When and where your funeral would be.
We would not have gone
But it would have been nice
To know when and where to grieve
If that feeling ever came to be.

We searched for your obituary
And read word for word
How you dotted on your wife,
That your dog was your life,
And that you happened to be survived
By your son,
His wife,
And those two kids you met
Less than five times in your life.

But by all means,
Go ahead and name-drop the dog
Instead of your so-called
"Family."
What a lasting memory to leave.
Perhaps that's what your tombstone should read,
"He had no more family to leave."

Penance

I did not do what you asked of me.
On your deathbed, I called,
Asking for an update.
You sounded unsteady,
Unlike yourself
But I did not know you that well
So who am I to tell?

You rambled on for a while
And before our time was through
You asked one thing,
"Pray for me, would you?"

It was a month later that you passed
And during all that time
I never once did what you asked.
I could not make myself do it.
I knew the words I'd use,
The requests I'd send to the powers that be,
Yet I chose to do nothing.

I felt nearly nothing
When I learned of your death.
But no matter what feelings I lacked.
I will forever be haunted by the fact
That I could not do
The bidding of a dying man.

I feel guilty.
Your last request was not

Too much to ask.

Still, I have not made up
For the time I chose not to act.

Dawn, Beyond, or Nothing at All

I'm keenly aware
That is the way I discuss death
If not the easiest to digest.
I acknowledge all ugly thoughts,
Bitter views, and sad remarks
All about someone
Who has passed on
To a glorious new dawn?
A fiery beyond?
Perhaps nothing at all.
Because I must tell the truth in Life,
For no one will be able to hear me screaming
In Death.

Hindsight

There is only one lesson
I wish I never learned:
A story
Will always end
Before you want it to.

You bought my words,
My stories and mistakes
So I'm sorry to say
This is where I leave you today.
Without a happy ending.
No matter how hard I try,
I do not think my words can provide you
With the ending you truly deserve.

I am not all-knowing, all-seeing,
Or even that bright.
I'm just a girl with a voice,
You, dear reader, are the one
That brings my stories to life.

A true conclusion starts with you,
Reading, thinking, feeling
As though my words do ring true.
All I am capable of is
Finishing this chapter,
This point in time with just us two,
In a way that will be memorable for both me
And you.

EPILOGUE

<u>listen to me</u>

"Who are you?"
This is the question I hate the most.
I find it impossible to answer.
At least with words.
Who are you?
Why do you care?
I know who I am in my heart.
I am me, just me.
That is the only answer you need.

It is a question,
I feel,
That has been romanticized to a damning extent.
If you cannot answer that question
Then you are incomplete.
You are valued less.
At least that's what we have been taught.

But why must we know?
Why does knowing
Make a person more valued?
More successful?
More whole?

So many people
Spend their lives,
Going mad trying to figure themselves out.
Because for some reason,
The world tells them they should.
That they need to,

They have to do so.

That question, that search,
Destroys the fabric of our beings.
As we look at ourselves
Through an analytical lens
In the search for an answer that people can accept,
We are only looking for the parts of us,
Real or fake,
That others can tolerate.

We know who we are deep down,
Whether we acknowledge It or not,
Whether we care or not.

Describing oneself
In a short sentence or two,
Is impossible.
We are indescribable.
Embarking on a never-ending journey
Every moment of our lives.

The question they crave the answer to,
Is not: who are you?
It is: who can you be for me?
It is an inquiry that I for one,
Do not want to answer.
I do not need to prove myself.
Or fit into a crowd of people
Who are so ready to annihilate themselves
To answer that question.

Because it is unnecessary.
Squeezing ourselves to fit in a mold,

Labeling ourselves so others
Have the opportunity to judge.
It will not work.
You are who you are
And I know who I am.
You do not need to answer that question,
Or discover your true self,
You already know.
You simply just need to be,
Be you.
That's all you need.

"Who are you?"
Good lord,

Who fucking cares.

Acknowledgments

I must start off once again by thanking my publishers at Wipf & Stock, for allowing me to continue writing, for myself and as my true self. To my friends who fed my ego more than they should have, I will always hold your compliments near and dear. And to my parents who unabashedly brag about their daughter the author, it is very cute but also so mortifying . . . I love you. To Ivette for creating concept sketches beyond my wildest dreams, your work inspired the cover art for not only *Growing Pains* but also my first book, *It Starts with the End*. I am immensely grateful for your art and friendship. Lastly, I need to thank the readers for indulging in my silly little endeavors and acknowledging a part of me that I thought would never be seen.

Made in the USA
Columbia, SC
14 October 2023

24450515R00063